# The Britain of Brian Cook

Stoke-by-Nayland, Suffolk

The artist in 1936

# The Britain of Brian Cook

by Brian Cook Batsford

Foreword by Sir Hugh Casson CH, KCVO, PPRA
Preface by Ian Logan FCSD

B.T. Batsford Ltd · London

ISBN 0 7134 5700 7

Typeset by Tek-Art Ltd, Kent
and printed in Hong Kong
by Bookbuilders Ltd
for the publishers
B.T. Batsford Ltd,
4 Fitzhardinge Street,
London W1H 0AH

# Foreword
## by Sir Hugh Casson CH KCVO PPRA

Anyone who was around in the world of architecture and landscape during the 'thirties' will remember the remarkable publications of Batsfords and the work of their talented young designer, Brian Cook. You could spot them a mile off . . . not just because of the 'Englishness' of the subject matter – villages, castles, churches, cottages and the countryside, but through the instantly recognisable strength of Brian Cook's dust jackets (the careful drawings, the large areas of flat, bright colours, the slightly hairy paper).

When looking at them again after 50 years they seem at first glance no more than charming period pieces, relics of a time when publishers sheltered behind Georgian sash windows, the word 'hype' had not been invented and (to begin with) there wasn't a paperback in sight. Yet, it would be a mistake – as Brian Cook records in this fascinating study – to treat them merely as curiosities, for at the time they were in the forefront in the arts and techniques of production and presentation and their young designer was a true pioneer, dealing on his own with everyone and everything – design, layout, materials, printing techniques, engravers and binders as well as editors and authors. No wonder today they are keenly collected as icons of their time. Brian Cook worked under difficulties and alone. His studio was a cramped suburban bedroom, his office an attic on the top floor of a rickety house supported, it appeared, entirely on loaded bookshelves. No consultants. No High Tech architecture. No Xerox, no promotional videos. Happier days? Maybe . . . Authors were perhaps less rich and famous, the speed of production less rapid, but more trouble was taken – or so it seems in retrospect – and there were fewer misprints and less aggro from the market.

But there is no trace of nostalgia in Brian Cook's account of his busy and inventive life, where single-handed he organized the appearance of so many books. Each had its own identity yet each was unmistakably part of the Batsford family and all of them were infused with their qualities – integrity, professionalism, consistency, radical ideas, lack of pretension. These are qualities always to be welcomed and treasured for today they are not often encountered. Here they are, recorded with modesty and providing a straight record of the aims, attitudes and techniques that helped to form Batsford's high reputation in the publishing world. It is the story of what was done and how it was done. Brian Cook obviously enjoyed every minute of it and in this book he sees to it that we enjoy it too.

DEDICATED
TO THE MEMORY OF
MY UNCLE HARRY BATSFORD
AND CHARLES FRY
PARTNERS IN THESE
PUBLISHING VENTURES

# Contents

# Acknowledgement

My first and major indebtedness is to B.T. Batsford Ltd for permission to reproduce so many of the book jackets designed for them from the early thirties to the early fifties. I would also like to thank Associated Book Publishers Ltd for permission to reproduce four of the fifteen or more covers for The Little Guides originally published by Messrs. Methuen and Co. Ltd and, for a period after the war, published jointly with B.T. Batsford Ltd; R.T. Tanner and Co. Ltd for permission to use the pen-and-ink drawing of St Paul's Cathedral on page 131.

I would also like to take this opportunity of expressing my debt to the many photographers whose work was used so extensively by Batsfords, before and after the war. I am especially grateful to the late Herbert Felton who was for long a personal friend and valued companion; Mr Will F. Taylor, a more prolific but subtler photographer of the landscape and Mr Brian C. Clayton whose collection of architectural detail was later purchased by Batsfords.

To them and others I am grateful for much reference material especially in connection with architectural detail and such complications as farm waggons and agricultural machinery. Their contribution towards these series of books has never been adequately acknowledged.

I wish to express my thanks to the late Francis Lucarotti, production manager at Batsfords from 1927 to 1954 who carefully stuck every new jacket into an album thus preserving them for all time and thereby enabling this book to be published.

Finally, I would like to thank Ian Jeffrey of The Arts Council, Ray Hallett of the National Trust and, above all, Ian Logan for the part they have played in this revival of my early work, which has made possible the publication of this book

BRIAN COOK BATSFORD

# Brian Cook
## by Ian Logan FCSD

The book jackets which form the major part of this book may represent Brian Cook's best known and easily recognized work as a designer, but, important as they are, they form a comparatively small part of his total output.

He started designing professionally in 1930, the same year that saw the founding of the Society of Industrial Artists. Brian was elected a Member six years later. The difference between the SIA then and the SCD, as we know it today, epitomizes the enormous changes in design management and its relationship with industry which have taken place during the last fifty years.

In the thirties, and certainly in the case of Batsfords, every aspect of the design of a book – cover, binding, title-page, text and illustration lay-out – was in the hands of one man who in turn was responsible for dealing with several trades – the paper-maker, printer (often more than one), engraver and binder, all of whom were involved in the production of a book.

Today a design department forms an essential part in almost every form of industry and publishers are no exception. The department may not even be part of the firm itself and the work may be farmed out to a firm of Design Consultants – a term unknown in the thirties. Brian Cook was fortunate in that his Uncle's publishing business already had an enviable reputation for good book production and presentation, though for strictly limited editions and a specialized market. But Brian introduced revolutionary changes in production and lay-out, many of which are

collector's items today. For the jacket of *The New Movement in the Theatre*, he worked with McKnight Kauffer whose design was screen-printed on thick cellophane enabling Brian's typography on a rough white canvas to show through. *Cecil Beaton's Scrapbook* (1937) involved three different coloured papers, letterpress, lithography and even collotype on which the text was printed in blue! *Cecil Beaton's New York* followed, a less flamboyant book, but Brian played great games with type and photographs, some of them significant steps in the art of typography.

I doubt if anyone can lay claim to be the first to use the 'bled-off' illustration but Brian was one of the earliest and seized the opportunity for *R.M.S. Queen Mary* published in a hurry to coincide with her maiden voyage in 1936. This was a stepping-stone in modern book production.

As Brian explains in his own introductory text, as a result of changing his name, his work under the name Brian Cook ceased to exist in the late forties. It was not until some forty years later that the flat-colour poster style of the thirties enjoyed a revival. Then these book jackets were plundered for stylish influence. Collected by designers like Allen Jones, George Hardie, Ian Beck and Glynn Boyd-Harte, they were hailed as part of a period style, the last phase, perhaps, of *Art Deco*. But nobody seemed to know whether the artist was alive or dead until he was unearthed by Ian Jeffries of the Arts Council and Ray Hallett of the National Trust.

Brian is rather surprised by this belated, and what he calls misplaced, recognition. That is understandable because the work of many artists, musicians or authors is often not recognised until long after their death. Few live to see their work acknowledged by succeeding generations. The reason in Brian's case is that his work was produced at an early age – most of it in his twenties, while many of his contemporaries in the poster style of that decade like Fred Taylor, Frank Newbould, Tom Purvis, Gregory Brown were of an earlier generation and have long since passed on. Yet, thankfully, in the world of design there are many pioneers still with us like Mylner Gray, Alec Games, Edward Bawden, S.R. Badmin and Robin Tanner. There is nothing surprising in the fact that almost all the work reproduced in these pages (which is only a fraction of his total output) should have been produced in the eight years between 1932 and 1940. This, in itself, is an achievement especially when it was a spare-time occupation.

There is already evidence that in his reluctant retirement, Brian Cook has been resuscitated and, in spite of his failing eyesight, carrying out several commissions. We can only speculate on what his contribution to British Design might have been if during the last forty years he had resisted the blandishments of Parliament.

## Illustrations in the introductory text

The pen-and-ink drawings reproduced in the introductory text appeared in the following early volumes: *The Villages of England* (1932); *The Landscape of England* (1933); *The Face of Scotland* (1933); *The Heart of Scotland* (1934); *The Old Inns of England* (1934) and *The Cathedrals of England* (1934).

# Introduction

## EARLY BACKGROUND

In any assessment of an artist's work, some reference to his background is relevant. Neither of my parents nor grandparents were artistically minded although my father did a little painting as a young man. One would need to go back two further generations to Raphael Angelo Turner, my great-grandmother's father and a colleague of George Morland, before claiming any hereditary talent.

I started to paint at Repton School during the four years from 1924 to 1928. When I had the customary farewell interview with the headmaster – Dr G.F. Fisher, subsequently Archbishop of Canterbury – he said, 'Well, Cook, all I can say about you is that, if nothing else, you have at least learnt to paint.' It was true: I had never passed any exams and have often since regretted my laziness in any subject but drawing. The art teaching at Repton was under the benevolent guidance of Arthur Norris, a son of a Dean of Westminster who, though no great painter himself, provided the facilities and encouragement which produced a succession of recognised artists: Anthony Gross, Rupert Shephard, Anthony Devas and my younger brother Neil, the most talented artist in our family. Neil went on to win a Scholarship in his first year at the Slade and was subsequently killed as a bomber pilot in 1941.

But the success of so many Repton painters in that decade was also due to the inspiration of a visiting teacher, Harold Gresley (1892-1967), who came from a well-known Derbyshire family of landscape painters. I have one of his father's watercolours and the Gresley technique in this painting of trees is clearly discernible in my study of willows by the River Trent of 1928 (page 33).

I find it more difficult to trace the architectural element in so much of my work. From an early age I visited old churches with my mother and even for a time shared her love of the Tudor and Elizabethan periods, but much as I wanted to be an architect, I could not have the necessary training and I can only attribute my interest to the countless books on architectural subjects published by the family firm of Batsford which must have been lying about at home.

The theory of perspective, essential to any architectural draftsman, somehow came naturally to me. The coloured pen-and-ink drawing of the Art School at Repton (page 12), done at the age of 16, was

The Art School, Repton
Coloured pen-and-ink drawing, 1927

completed in strips from top to bottom without any conscious recognition of the rules of perspective – and no doubt to the exasperation of my teachers. This drawing was followed a year later (1928) by a detailed study of the Sixth Form Room (now the Audit Room) reproduced on page 36.

It was inevitable, as the time came for me to leave school, that I should urge my parents to allow me to take up art as a career. There was never any question of their being able to afford this but they did take me round to various well-known artists of the day – mostly Academicians – to ask for their opinion, which was not very conclusive. Eventually it was agreed that I should go into the family bookselling and publishing business of Batsford with its shop in High Holborn and, as a concession, also attend the Central School of Arts and Crafts in Southampton Row around the corner. I was taken to see the then headmaster who looked at my work and remarked, 'Now you must forget all this and start all over again.' So I found myself re-drawing plaster casts under John Farleigh; writing Gothic script under Noel Rooke; and life-drawing under somebody else. The difficulty of only attending in the afternoons was that you always arrived half-way through, with the result that the life classes in particular were rarely worthwhile. Before long I returned

full-time to publishing and later much regretted that this academic training, especially in figure drawing, was so curtailed. When I returned to the Central, as a Governor, nearly 50 years later, it had become rather a different type of school, and large abstracts were the order of the day.

## PUBLISHING

My first few years at Batsfords were spent in an eighteenth-century building in Holborn which was reputedly held up only by the shelves of books in every room. The production department, the staff of which was increased to four by my arrival, worked in an attic 12 ft square beneath a ceiling 7 ft high (I am 6 ft 4 ins). There was one small window overlooking the chimney pots of Red Lion Square. Everybody in the room smoked. But it was there that I learnt the intricacies of the various processes of reproduction: letterpress, photogravure, lithography and even collotype; and the names and sizes of typefaces, the weight and texture of paper. An education which, supplemented by practical experience outside, I still find invaluable nearly 60 years later.

Above: colophon designed by Kruger Gray in 1930 to symbolize the succession of booksellers in High Holborn since 1611

Right: view from the production department at High Holborn

Although organized in these squalid and cramped conditions, the firm's products maintained a high standard and I remember with pride the work first entrusted to me: the division into two volumes of *The Domestic Architecture of the Tudor Period* by Garner and Stratton. The two folio volumes had a deep-red wrapper to match the buckram binding on which, in addition to the title and authors' names, was embossed a Tudor medallion designed by Kruger Gray, then designer of a new set of coins of the realm.

## THE ENGLISH LIFE SERIES

This was generally the pattern of what in those days were known as 'wrappers' or 'dust covers': a printed version of the lettering, and possibly colophon, which was embossed in gold leaf on the binding of the book itself. This, with very few exceptions, was the style followed until the late twenties when Batsford introduced their so-called *English Life Series*. This originally comprised five volumes: *The English Countryside* and *English Country Life and Work* by Ernest Pulbrook; *Old English Household Life* by Gertrude Jekyll – better known for her books on gardening; *The English Cottage* by Basil Oliver and *The English Inn, Past and Present* by A.E. Richardson.

For this series Batsford introduced what was for them a new type of wrapper and commissioned such artists as Gregory Brown and Fred Taylor, both well known as poster designers for the Railways and London's 'Underground'.

The illustration was restricted to the front and possibly the spine of the book only. The back was left blank and usually being white was soon apt to get dirty. As a further volume in this series, an Eton master, A.K. Wickham, was invited to write the text for a book entitled *The Villages of England*. It was for this book, published in 1932, that I designed my first wrapper (pages 15 and 45).

94 High Holborn in the 'twenties

The jacket itself (I propose to use the customary word jacket from here on) was different in many respects from all previous Batsford jackets:

a   The design wrapped right round the book – i.e. the picture covered all three sections of the jacket: front, spine and back.

b   It was 'bled off', i.e. there was no white frame or margin to the design – it ran over the edge in every direction: top, bottom and sides.

c   It was printed by an unfamiliar colour process.

d   The book was easier to handle because the design was printed on rough paper which did not slip like the previous 'shiny' art paper.

e   For the same reason it fitted the book more snugly, was less likely to fall off and, as a result, became more part of the book itself.

f   The colours used in the design were, for those days, blatant, bizarre, strident and unreal.

I make no claim that the jacket for *The Villages of England* was the first design to wrap right around the book, nor the first jacket to bleed off. The history of book jacket design goes back to the middle of the last century and ever since then publishers have been experimenting with different forms of book cover either on the book itself or on the paper cover originally designed to keep it clean in the bookseller's shop.

Undoubtedly the most important and most obvious difference between this and all previous jackets was the brilliance of colour. This, in turn was due to the use of a special printing process: Jean Berté. This almost unique method of printing is described on page 39.

The first Brian Cook jacket – designed to wrap right round the book

Cottages at Lavenham, Suffolk, from *The Villages of England*, 1932

The church tower at Huish Episcopi, Somerset, from *The Villages of England*, 1932

Opposite, left: old houses and the Abbey Tower, Tewkesbury: pen-and-ink drawing for *The Landscape of England*, 1933

Opposite, right: the River Severn at Bridgnorth, Shropshire: tinted pencil drawing for the colour frontispiece of *The Landscape of England*, 1933

The financial crisis of 1929/31 seriously affected the publishing trade and for Batsford it came immediately after an expensive move into more spacious premises in the West End. We were forced to go through the painful business of reducing staff while Harry Batsford, the Company Chairman, determined to introduce the strictest economies, decided to dispense with the services of authors and illustrators. He and Charles Fry, the principal editor, would write the books, I would help find the illustrations, do any black-and-white drawings and design the jackets – as well as design the book itself.

As we were determined to continue publishing books on the English countryside, *The Villages of England* was followed by *The Homes and Gardens of England* by Batsford and Fry and *The Landscape of England* by the same authors but under the pseudonym of Charles Bradley Ford.

The jackets of both of these books were printed by the Jean Berté process. Nevertheless, I was struggling to find a more satisfactory colour formula as is evident in the jackets themselves (pages 46 & 47) which show a marked contrast in style. In *The Landscape of England* the jacket comprised a view of the coastline at Coombe Martin in Devon and in the valley behind I had inserted a Cotswold church tower and village to provide interest on the front of the book. Fifty years later the original was exhibited by the Arts Council in their 1983 exhibition at the Hayward Gallery of 'English Landscape Painting 1850-1950'.

Canterbury Cathedral from the south-west

Portsee Harbour, Isle of Skye

Harry Batsford, Charles Fry and the Morris at the top of Gruinard Hill, then one of the steepest gradients in Scotland

## THE BRITISH HERITAGE SERIES

In April 1933 the triumvirate of Batsford, Fry and Cook toured Scotland in a Morris Oxford for three weeks and on their return produced *The Face of Scotland* (page 49). This was a landmark in pre-war publishing because we were determined to abandon the old format of *The English Life Series*, published at 12/6d, and produce a smaller (Demy 8vo) book with 128 pages of text, over 100 photographs, many line drawings and a coloured jacket for the price of an ordinary novel; namely 7/6d (about 40p in today's currency although very much more in real terms). To achieve this necessitated a gamble involving a print number of 8500 copies. The book was an immediate success and became the first volume of what we named *The British Heritage Series. The Face of Scotland* was reprinted at least four times. It was also important so far as the jacket was concerned. I had evolved a colour sequence which was used for all other volumes in the series and which is illustrated on page 39.

*The British Heritage Series*, firmly established in its permanent format, provided me with the opportunity of designing nearly 30 book jackets all printed by the Jean Berté process.

Regent Arch, Edinburgh, from *The Heart of Scotland*, 1934

St Andrews, from *The Face of Scotland*, 1933

20

Forres, from *The Heart of Scotland*, 1934

**Eight drawings of detail from *The Cathedrals of England*, 1934**

Romanesque capital in the crypt, Canterbury Cathedral

Spandrel carving, the expulsion from Eden, in the Angel Choir, Lincoln Cathedral

The tomb of Abbot Newland in the Lady Chapel, Bristol Cathedral

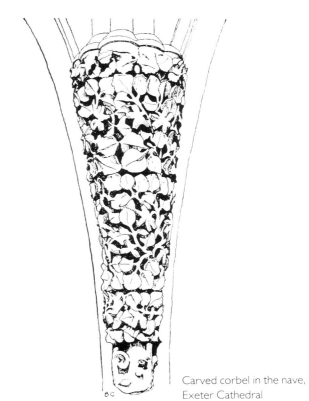

Carved corbel in the nave, Exeter Cathedral

22

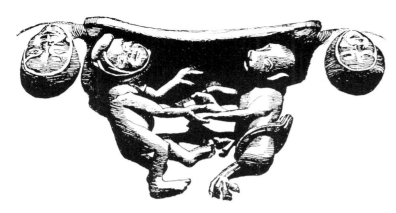

Misericord, Chichester Cathedral

Carved boss, the murder of Becket, in the nave vault, Exeter Cathedral

Romanesque carving of the Prior's Door, Ely Cathedral

The Prior's Door in the cloisters, Norwich Cathedral

23

*The British Heritage Series* had purposely covered the more tangible aspects of the English countryside, in particular the man-made features of our heritage: the cathedrals, churches, castles, villages, cottages of Britain.

Its companion series *The Face of Britain* was designed to describe aspects of the countryside on a geographical basis. I would have liked it planned county by county but Harry Batsford favoured areas like 'The Cotswolds' or 'The Chilterns' and that became the pattern which was followed. The two series were published concurrently; their format and number of illustrations were the same. But we made one major change: for the jackets of *The Face of Britain Series* we deserted the Jean Berté process and used photolithography.

I had begun to resent the restrictions imposed by flat colour and personally disliked the idea of depicting the English heritage in colours which were, to me, harsh and unreal. I felt rather ashamed that I had portrayed the tower of Gloucester Cathedral in the colours of the rainbow or the old cottages in Kersey in a series of brilliant purples; although this interpretation may now be acclaimed by some. So, rather to my relief, the new series was presented in more natural colours photographically reproduced and printed by lithography – though I hoped that some of the brightness and colour of the previous series would be maintained. The first two volumes, *English Downland* (1936) (p.82) and *The Highlands of Scotland* (p.83) (1936), were both in fact painted in oils. After this I switched to what I called 'body-colour', a technique now more commonly referred to as 'gouache'.

*The Face of Britain Series* ultimately ran to 24 volumes, a few of them published as late as 1950, and in order to keep the series uniform my designs were used for the jackets.

Above: Stoke Gabriel on the Dart, South Devon

Richmond Castle and the River Swale, Yorkshire

Carved wordwork windows at the back of The Luttrell Arms,
Dunster, Somerset

Staircase in the yard of the former Plume of Feathers, Salisbury, Wiltshire

The North Devon coast looking west to Hartland Point, watercolour, 1945

Looking towards the Lizard from Mullion, Cornwall, watercolour, 1946

**A selection of pub interiors, two of them no longer identifiable**

The old chimney corner at The Union Inn, Flyford Flavell, Worcestershire

The tap-room fireplace at The White Hart, Bletchingley, Surrey

The bar-parlour of The Trout at Godstow

A chimney-corner at The White Horse, Eaton Socon, Bedfordshire

The Pomfret Arms, Towcester, Northamptonshire

The landscapes and townscapes which provided jacket material for the 50-plus volumes of the main series of books on the countryside are those which to pre-war generations meant 'Batsford Books' and the image was created not only by the uniformity of design and format but by the words '*A Batsford Book*' which we printed on the front flap of every jacket. This was a good example of 'selling the firm and not the product' which obviously paid dividends in a small firm such as ours, and is maintained to this day.

But there were many other books outside the two main series which covered other aspects of the countryside but which were produced in a variety of styles and sizes. The size was reduced and the price was cut to five shillings for what was rather pompously named *The Pilgrim's Library*, which consisted of a series of articles by various authors but which only achieved three volumes: *The Beauty of Britain* had two jackets, one designed by Fred Taylor and the other, in Jean Berté, by me (page 78). The second, *The Legacy of England*, was again an anthology but with a jacket reproduced from scraperboard over-printed in black on top of Jean Berté (page 79). The third was *Nature in Britain* by Frances Pitt (page 105).

H.L. Edlin, the authority on trees, was commissioned to do *British Woodland Trees*, and *Forestry and Woodland Life*. These encouraged a certain amount of experiment in jacket design. For *English Woodland* by John Rodgers (page 113) I had kept to pure watercolour and was obviously influenced by the work of Ethelbert White. In *British Woodland Trees* (page 114) I experimented with creating a space for the title in the design itself which was not altogether successful.

Edlin continued to write for Batsford and produced *British Plants and Their Uses* which must have been one of the last Jean Berté jackets; in this case heavily over-printed by a detailed half-tone drawing – a technique I was to employ with a series of small books on Cathedral Cities after the war, which was, in fact, the farewell to the Jean Berté process, as least so far as we were concerned.

The George, Glastonbury, formerly The Pilgrim's Inn; from *The Old Inns of England*, 1934

A few of the later books – some of them increased in size and price – grouped themselves together like A.G. Street's *Farming England*, Sir William Beach-Thomas's *Hunting England* and Patrick Chalmers's *Racing England* which formed an interesting trio. Many others are illustrated on these pages and listed in the catalogue at the end. They carried on the Batsford tradition throughout the thirties and later, and succeeded in providing the reading public with a worthwhile text and a large number of good illustrations for a very reasonable price. The colourful jacket probably did no more than attract attention in the bookshop window.

Lincoln Cathedral from the Witham; from *The Landscape of England*, 1933

Catalogue cover, scraperboard, *c.* 1939

The River Trent at Repton, Derby,
watercolour 1928; see text on page 11.

# SOME PRINCIPLES OF BOOK JACKET DESIGN

An 'overall' book jacket – for want of a better term – in fact comprises four separate designs: 1. the front cover; 2. the back cover; 3. the spine (the only exposed portion when a book is on the shelf); and 4. the whole design (see opposite).

In fact the first three elements are the only ones seen with any frequency: the front when it is displayed in the bookshop window, on the bookshop table or on the table at home; the spine when it is in its proper and possibly final place, on the shelf; the back only when it is accidentally left upside down. The whole design – although it may have involved the greatest concern with the designer – is rarely, if ever, seen. The purchaser of a book may take off the jacket to see the whole effect, then promptly put it back – or glance at it briefly before discarding the jacket into the waste-paper basket while putting the book on the shelf.

The whole all-over design, therefore, often without its lettering, finds its permanent home in the publisher's archives, or now more often the artist's home, a work of art only to be seen publicly in its triple state or as a slowly fading strip on the shelf. The jackets illustrated here, therefore, are mostly being seen – at least by younger generations – for the first time in their original and complete form.

In a few cases more than one jacket was designed for the same title. *The English Abbey* and *The Parish Churches of England* were the only examples of this in *The British Heritage Series*. I remember that I always disliked the first jacket for *Parish Churches* (page 54) and for a later edition designed a new cover (page 55) which I think I dislike even more.

I have no idea, however, why I should have replaced the original jacket of *The English Abbey* (page 56) with the indifferent and more distant view of Llanthony Abbey (page 57) unless it was on instructions from my uncle, Harry Batsford, who had an obsession with the latter where he spent many weeks every year.

In my early days of publishing, immense trouble was taken with the design of the binding of the book – as indeed had been the case ever since books were first produced. The title of the book was embossed, usually in gold leaf, on the front of the book, often accompanied by some sort of colophon or heraldic device. For one of the first books I remember handling, *Spanish Gardens*, I had to produce a design for the front of the binding in three or more colours. To repeat this on a matching paper jacket seemed an unnecessary extravagance.

When *The British Heritage Series* was first introduced, and many economies made in production in order to keep the retail price low, one of the first parts of the book to suffer was the cloth binding. Buckram was replaced with a cheap canvas; all lettering on the side (or front) of the book was dispensed with. The lettering on the spine lost all its silver or gold and became plain blocking in a colour to tone with that of the binding.

As I took home a copy of every book we published – in pre-war years this would be only about 50 or 60 a year – I automatically removed the jacket and threw it away as I thought that books looked best on their shelf with only the dark colours of their bindings visible. This was a familiar practice at the time. But the plain backs and the sans-serif lettering on the new Batsford series looked rather dull. Worse was to come: the binding cloth was of poor quality and started to fade and in many cases the lettering became illegible.

To get over this in the fifties and sixties I re-introduced gold for the title on the spine and added a series of double bands down the whole length of the spine. This was intended as a distinguishing trade mark for all Batsford books on a library shelf. But it was, of course, a wasted effort as, in the event, people kept the jacket on the books and their secondhand value is greater with the jackets than without.

The jacket of *The Countryman's England*, 1935, divided to show the three basic
components: front, back and spine, each requiring a separate pictorial composition yet
forming an embracing composition for the whole design. The drawing also
incorporated allowances for 'bleed' at the top, bottom and sides

The Sixth Form Room at Repton (now called the Audit Room); pen-and-ink and watercolour, 1928. The original of this drawing now hangs in the room

36

**Ground**  Almost without exception all the book jacket originals were painted on Whatman Water-colour Board (NOT SURFACE) manufactured by Winsor and Newton Limited. I have always found this surface sympathetic to painting in watercolour or gouache.

**Size and scale**  As far as size was concerned any jacket designed for reproduction by the Jean Berté process had to be exactly the same size (S/S). This was essential so that an accurate tracing could be made for the rubber blocks.

The majority of the jackets were for *The British Heritage Series* and *The Face of Britain Series*, size Demy 8vo (8¾ in deep by 5⅝ in wide). Therefore allowing ¼ in for bleed on top and bottom and ½ in for wrap-round on to the jacket flaps, the original was almost invariably 9¼ in by 11¼ in to which had to be added the width of the spine. As most of the books comprised 128 pages of text (one sheet of paper per book) and 96 pages of plates on art paper, the spine width was fairly constant.

If the books were to look worth their price (7s 6d) a certain degree of bulk was considered essential. This was achieved by printing the text on Antique Wove – a little too much like blotting paper for my line drawings; and often also – most unethical in my view – by binding in at the end of the book a 32-page catalogue of the firm's publications.

**Paints**  As a general rule I used watercolours in tubes mixed with Chinese White (except when I used the actual watercolour printing ink). As the Jean Berté process demanded the use of flat colour, this mixture was essential and no graduation in colour was feasible. I always called this type of paint 'body-colour' and still do – although various manufacturers have since put on the market what they call 'poster colour' which, I assume, is the same thing. Now, of course, we are familiar with 'gouache', a very old name for a type of painting which has been more familiar, and certainly popular, in recent years. However, my original mixture of watercolour and Chinese White has the major disadvantage of drying several shades darker than when the colour is first applied. It was,

'The Artist at Bay', 1972, by Sir Hugh Casson, CH, KCVO, PPRA

therefore, always essential – and still is with modern materials – to have a testing board close at hand and wait for the colour to dry before applying it to the painting.

As I had worked out a colour scheme involving four printings, giving 14 different colours, I would mix up quantities of these colours in china palettes, or white saucers, which were almost invariably sufficient for the complete job. This saved a lot of time because colour mixed in this way can always be worked up again, with a small addition of water, after it has dried.

Flower arrangement designed to illustrate the versitility of the Jean Berté process, c. 1935

Pre-war cover of the Heidelberg House Magazine, which featured the Jean Berté process

# THE JEAN BERTÉ PROCESS

I do not remember how I was first introduced to the Jean Berté method of printing. Presumably a representative of the printers using it called in 1930 or '31 with specimens and we decided to make an experiment.

The Jean Berté process may have evolved as a result of numerous efforts to emulate the French hand-stencil process of watercolour printing. The process is primarily a letterpress printing method employing resilient-surfaced rubber plates, rubber rollers and watercolour inks of high intensity.

The principal characteristic of the process was this use of water-based, as opposed to oil-based, inks; a distinction with which we are now familiar in artists' colours (oil or acrylic) or in decorators' paints (oil-based or water-based/emulsion).

Jean Berté printing can be done on any type of letterpress machine (we used a Victoria Platten or Super-speed Heidelberg) and the only change necessary on the machine was the substitution of resilient rubber rollers which are essential to watercolour printing. The inks are much more brilliant than oil inks and as they do not contain varnish or dryers many combinations of colour effects can be obtained by overlapping: soft matt colours in a variety of rich, pure shades. Thus it is possible to obtain three colours with two workings, seven with three workings, fourteen colours with four workings and so on. A slight variant on this pattern, using more subtle colours, was used for jackets such as that illustrated on page 41.

The rubber plates – usually four – are cut by hand. A tracing is made on thick cellophane from the artist's original design and this is impressed on the rubber plate – usually by rubbing red ink into the grooves on the cellophane. Each portion of the rubber block which is not required in the respective colour is marked with red ink and subsequently cut out by a scalpel.

As can be imagined, this required great skill and care in view of the 14 different colours obtained by over-printing. It was not a simple process in other respects. The strength or intensity of colour used on the

Jean Berté colour chart: the three primary colours, and grey. A fifth printing of black was added for emphasis

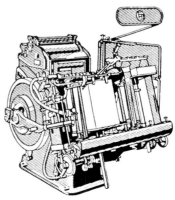

The Super-Speed Heidelberg

machine could produce a variety of different effects quite unintended in the original drawing. If I remember correctly, the colours were printed in the order: blue, red, yellow and grey. As the title of the books was printed in black it enabled me to introduce a fifth printing and an important part of the design was provided by the extra emphasis which black gave as part of it. The depth of the yellow and grey were very important because they controlled all the deeper colours in the design.

For this reason, I always went to the printers, Messrs. Herbert Reiach Ltd, to supervise the job on the machine so that if the result was unsatisfactory, it was my fault and not theirs. The works were situated at 43 Belvedere Road, London S.E.1, in a rather derelict area between Waterloo Station and the Thames; the spot where the jackets for *The British Heritage Series* were printed was approximately where the Royal Festival Hall now stands.

## SOURCE MATERIAL

The book jackets illustrated here were all, without exception, designed and carried out 'in the studio'. The studio in my case throughout the period 1932 to 1940 was a small bedroom in a suburban home near London.

The jacket designs were prepared from a number of different sources: pencil sketches made on the spot, my own photographs and those by other, usually professional, photographers.

I do not like working from photographs – certainly not unless they are my own, where I have been responsible for the composition. It is not generally realized how much photographs distort. A distant hill or mountain is often reduced in height photographically. Nowadays, of course, there may be means of correcting this, but generally speaking what the camera sees in a landscape is very different from the human eye. This was certainly true fifty years ago.

*London Historic Buildings*, uniform volume with *London Work and Play* (opposite)

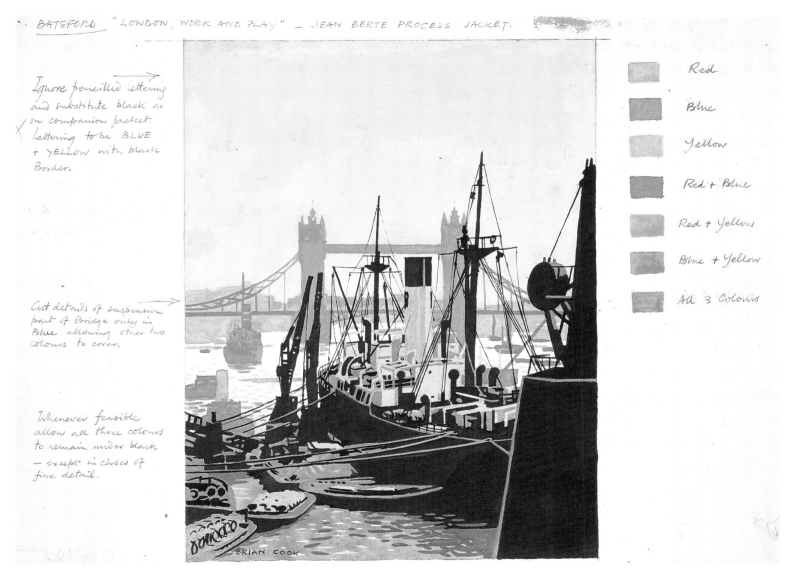

BATSFORD "LONDON, WORK AND PLAY" — JEAN BERTÉ PROCESS JACKET.

Ignore pencilled lettering
and substitute black as
on companion jacket.
Lettering to be BLUE
+ YELLOW with black
Border.

Cut details of suspension
part of Bridge only in
Blue allowing other two
colours to cover.

Whenever feasible
allow all three colours
to remain under black
— except in cases of
fine detail.

Red.
Blue
Yellow
Red + Blue
Red + Yellow
Blue + Yellow
All 3 Colours

BRIAN COOK

*London: Work and Play*, a later variant using more subdued colours by the same process

But nothing can compete with the pleasure of working in the open air – even with all the discomforts of wind and cold or the hazards of changing light.

The great majority of the jackets, unless they portrayed an individual building such as Gloucester Cathedral (page 50) were designed from a number of different photographs and especially portions of photographs to provide suitable compositions for the three elements of the jacket: front, back and spine (as described on page 34).

Batsford had a large collection of architectural and topographical photographs collected over a period of years: many since before the First World War. This provided a source of photographs of villages, churches, cottages and landscape which could be incorporated in a design. In addition I kept at home drawers full of illustrations torn out of newspapers and magazines which provided foreground material, especially figures, horses, farm vehicles and even cars. All this was necessary to enable me to work out of office hours and late at night.

Probably the most important point to remember about the work of landscape painters, poster artists and book-jacket designers of fifty years ago is that there was no such thing as colour photography – except for pioneers experimenting in this field. This fact comes as a surprise to modern generations who nowadays take such things for granted. But what it meant to the landscape artist – especially those confined to a studio – was that one essential qualification was a detailed knowledge and appreciation of the colour of the British countryside and of building materials, even though many liberties were taken with colour exaggeration.

## THE END OF A CHAPTER

Most of these book jackets belong to a distinct period: the eight years between 1932 and 1940. They belong to the thirties and to the period now known as *Art Deco*.

Their design and production did not end abruptly because, as I have said

earlier, a few isolated volumes in *The Face of Britain Series* were published as late as 1950 and, to preserve the continuity, I designed the jacket. A few, such as John Russell's *Shakespeare's Country*, were designed when I was home on leave from the RAF and this particular jacket (page 94), for reasons of economy, only had a pictorial front and spine.

There were a number of reasons why the Brian Cook jackets came to a fairly abrupt end: the war, the advent of colour photography and, most important of all, because the artist ceased to paint under that name.

I remember being very excited about the coming of colour photography. After producing every book illustrated by black-and-white photographs it would be revolutionary to have even some of them in colour. My Uncle, Harry Batsford, who could make no claim as a photographer, would load his box camera with *Dufaycolor* film and rush off to the Cotswolds. The results (very small and out of focus) were actually published in a book called *The Coloured Counties* for which the text was written in the office. It was a dismal failure and was, I believe, re-issued under another title *England in Colour* for which I designed another jacket (page 136), presumably in the hope that potential buyers might think it was a different book. The only photographer of landscape in colour whom I recall from those pre-war days was F.R. Newens of Oxford and by the standards of the time his work was superb.

It is difficult to pin-point the precise post-war years when colour photography gradually approached its present day standards but it was used automatically for the jackets of our topographical books from the middle or late fifties, slowly reaching the high standards of today. There was, however, one fundamental difference so far as Batsford jackets were concerned: the back of the book was, in future for a time, always plain.

Publishing was drastically reduced during the war primarily as a result of the shortage of paper. The Government also introduced strict economy standards of production. Batsford evacuated to Malvern in 1939 even before the war started. This move, prompted by an exaggerated fear of what bombs would do to London, ultimately enabled my Uncle and a

*North Oxford Cedar*, one of the last Brian Cook paintings. Oil, *c.* 1946

skeleton staff to enjoy more than ten years in the country. In fact, the book trade was hit worse than most although Batsford's London office remained intact throughout.

At the end of the war when paper was scarce and book production at a low ebb, Batsford suddenly released on to the market thousands of copies of *The Heritage of Britain Series* and *The Face of Britain Series*, much to the surprise of the book trade. My Uncle had ordered the reprinting of all these titles in the early days of the war when we held stocks of paper. Then, to use his own words, he 'put them into cold storage' for the duration. Thus a famous series which had really come to an end in 1939 was still flourishing seven years later.

There is no need to dwell at any length on the most obvious reason for the comparatively sudden end to the work of Brian Cook as a designer of book jackets – or indeed any other form of designing. In June 1946 at my Uncle's request and by deed poll, I added my Mother's name of Batsford to my own in order to ensure the retention of the name in the family business then over a century old. This, as it turned out, was only a temporary expedient which lasted for the years of my Chairmanship from 1952 to 1974 as I, like Harry Batsford, have no male heir.

It also involved starting a new career. The use of the name Brian Batsford, until then unknown, unintentionally but irrevocably put an end at the age of 35 to the work of Brian Cook, the artist.

The book jackets which are reproduced in the pages which follow appear, as far as possible, in chronological order. In some cases their precise date of publication is not known. An exception to this rule has, occasionally, been made in order to keep well-known series together in spite of the fact that their dates of production overlapped.

This book has only been made possible as a result of the careful collection of mint copies of most of the printed jackets and the discovery, about ten years ago, of a little more than half of the original paintings.

In all I designed about 150 book jackets, the great majority of them for B.T. Batsford Limited and it is those which were produced for the books on British topography – nearly 100 in all – which are reproduced here.

The great majority of the jackets were done during the years 1932 to 1940, virtually half a century ago. It is probably not surprising that 36 of the original designs are regrettably missing; only a few were given away, but I might have taken greater care of them had I known that one day they could be recognised as a contribution to British design of the thirties.

The selection of those for reproduction in colour has been governed entirely by whether the original or the jacket (with its inevitable panels of lettering) was of the better quality. In many cases the original had faded, or the only jacket available had been round a book for several years with plenty of wear and tear.

It has been surprising to find that after fifty years one still has a memory for titles, author's names and even places but that has not prevented a considerable amount of research which has, I hope, made this collection complete.

For those, both in Britain and America, who have been making a collection of these books, preferably, I understand, with the jacket still intact, there is a Collectors' Checklist at the end of the book. I wish them every success in their endeavours and am flattered by their interest.

## THE ENGLISH LIFE SERIES

**The Villages of England**
by A.K. Wickham, Large 8vo, 1932.
The first jacket designed by Brian Cook and the first to be reproduced for Batsford by the Jean Berté process

*The village of Kersey in Suffolk*

BRIAN COOK 1932

**The Homes and Gardens of England**
by Harry Batsford and Charles Fry, Large 8vo, 1932

*The house and garden, St Catherine's Court, Somerset*

46

THE LAND-SCAPE OF ENG-LAND FORD

THE LANDSCAPE OF ENGLAND

BATS-FORD

**The Landscape of England**
by Charles Bradley Ford, Large 8vo, 1933.
Exhibited with the original at the Arts Council Exhibition 'Landscape in Britain 1850-1950', Hayward Gallery, April 1983

*An imaginary coastal scene based on the headlands of Great and Little Hangman, North Devon*

# THE BRITISH HERITAGE SERIES

Unless stated otherwise the size of all the books is Demy 8vo.

A publicity photograph for *The British Heritage Series. Circa* 1937, when smoking was evidently still fashionable

**The Face of Scotland**
by Harry Batsford and Charles Fry, 1933.
The first volume in *The British Heritage Series*       *An imaginary Scottish scene incorporating Eilean Donan Castle*

**The Cathedrals of England**

by Harry Batsford and Charles Fry, 1934     *Gloucester Cathedral from the south-east*

**The Heart of Scotland** by George Blake, 1934
*A Scottish fishing village based on Crail, Fife*

**English Villages and Hamlets**
by Humphrey Pakington, 1934    *Based on the village of Ruardean, Gloucestershire*

**The Old Inns of England**
by A.E. Richardson, 1934    *Based on The Old Bell at Hurley, Berkshire*

**The Parish Churches of England**
by The Reverend J.C. Cox and Charles Bradley Ford, 1935

THE
PARISH
CHURCHES
OF
ENGLAND

COX
AND
FORD

PARISH CHURCHES
OF ENGLAND

BATS-
FORD

BRIAN COOK

**The Parish Churches of England**
A later jacket for the same volume

**The English Abbey**
by F.H. Crossley, 1935    *Whitby Abbey, Yorkshire*

**The English Abbey**
A later jacket for the same volume *Llanthony Abbey, Monmouthshire (now Gwent)*

**The English Country House**

by Ralph Dutton, 1935    *Based on Owlpen Manor, Gloucestershire*

**The English Garden**
by Ralph Dutton, 1937   *The garden at Canons Ashby, Northamptonshire*

**The English Castle**
by Hugh Braun, 1936

*Ludlow Castle, Shropshire*

THE OLD PUBLIC SCHOOLS OF ENGLAND

RODGERS

OLD PUBLIC SCHOOLS OF ENGLAND

BATS-FORD

JOHN RODGERS

**The Old Public Schools of England**
by John Rodgers, 1938

*Eton College: School Yard and Lupton's tower*

THE
SEAS
AND
SHORES
OF
ENG-
LAND

VALE

SEAS AND SHORES
OF ENGLAND

BATS-
FORD

BRIAN
COOK

EDMUND VALE

**The Seas and Shores of England**
by Edmund Vale, 1936

**The Countryman's England**
by Dorothy Hartley, 1935

**The Old Towns of England**
by Clive Rouse, 1936

*The market at Cirencester, Gloucestershire*

64

**The Heart of England**
by Ivor Brown, 1935

*The front at Brighton, Sussex, with the Metropole Hotel*

ENGLISH
VILLAGE
HOMES

SYDNEY
R.
JONES

ENGLISH VILLAGE
HOMES

BATS-
FORD

SYDNEY R. JONES

BRIAN COOK

**English Village Homes**
by Sydney R. Jones, 1936    *An adaptation of Mere, Wiltshire*

**The English Cottage**
by Harry Batsford and Charles Fry, 1938    *A cottage at Bignor, Sussex*

**The Land of Wales**
by Eiluned and Peter Lewis, 1937

**The Spirit of Ireland**
by Lynn Doyle, 1935

**Old English Customs and Ceremonies**
by F.J. Drake-Carnell, 1938

*The Changing of the Guard at the Horse Guards, Whitehall*

**The Spirit of London**
by Paul Cohen-Portheim, 1935

*Ludgate Circus and St Paul's*

**Prehistoric England**
by Grahame Clark, 1940

*Maiden Castle from an aerial photograph*

**British Hills and Mountains**
by J.H.B. Bell, E.F. Bozman and J. Fairfax Blakeborough, 1940

**Old English Household Life**
by Gertrude Jekyll and Sydney R. Jones, 1939.
A revision of Miss Jekyll's book of the same title originally published in the twenties

**English Church Design**
by F.H. Crossley, 1945

*The church at Terrington St Clement, Norfolk*

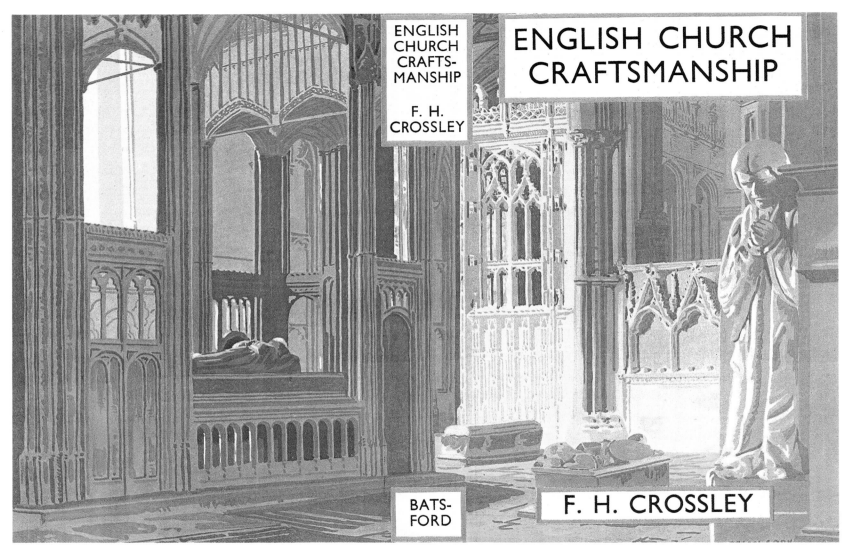

**English Church Craftsmanship**
by F.H. Crossley, 1941

*The Retro-Quire, Winchester Cathedral*

**The Greater English Church**
by Harry Batsford and Charles Fry, 1940

*The Nave of York Minster with the Quire beyond*

**The Beauty of Britain**
by J.B. Priestley and others, Crown 8vo, 1935

*An imaginary landscape*

**The Legacy of England**
A collection of essays, Crown 8vo, 1935.
Scraper board overprinted on Jean Berté

*Adapted from Castle Combe, Wiltshire*

A CATALOGUE
OF BOOKS

BATSFORD'S ILLUSTRATED CATALOGUE OF PUBLICATIONS ON ART, ARCHITECTURE, SOCIAL LIFE, ETC.

15 NORTH AUDLEY STREET, LONDON, W.I

B. T. BATSFORD LTD.

BRIAN COOK

THE FACE OF BRITAIN SERIES

All Demy 8vo and printed by offset lithography unless otherwise stated; the original paintings were, unless otherwise stated, executed in what is now known as 'gouache'.

**Cover for a General Catalogue**
*Circa* 1937.
Pen-and-ink over-printed on Jean Berté

*An imaginary English village from the air*

**Autumn List cover**
*Circa* 1939.
Printed in three-colour line

THE
ENG-
LISH
DOWN-
LAND

Massing
-ham

THE FACE OF BRITAIN

# ENGLISH DOWNLAND
### By H. J. Massingham

BATSFORD

BRIAN COOK

**The English Downland**
by H.J. Massingham, 1936
Original painted in oils

*An imaginary Sussex Downland scene*

THE
HIGH-
LANDS
OF
SCOT-
LAND

Quigley
★
Adam

THE FACE OF BRITAIN

# THE HIGHLANDS
# OF SCOTLAND

By Hugh Quigley

BATSFORD

With Photographs by ROBERT M. ADAM

BRIAN COOK

**The Highlands of Scotland**
by Hugh Quigley, 1936
Painted in oils

*Gruinard Bay, Ross and Cromarty*

**Cotswold Country**

by H.J. Massingham, 1937

NORTH
COUN-
TRY

Vale

THE FACE OF BRITAIN

NORTH
COUNTRY
By Edmund Vale

BATSFORD

**North Country**
by Edmund Vale, 1937

*The village of Muker in Upper Swaledale, Yorkshire*

THE
FACE
OF
IRE-
LAND

Floyd

THE FACE OF
IRELAND
By Michael Floyd

BATSFORD

**The Face of Ireland**
by Michael Floyd, 1937

**The Lowlands of Scotland**
by George Scott-Moncrieff, 1939

WEST
COUNTRY

# WEST COUNTRY

## C. HENRY WARREN

C.
HENRY
WARREN

BATSFORD

**West Country**
by C. Henry Warren, 1938
Watercolour

*The village of Sheepwash, North Devon*

**Welsh Border Country**
by P. Thoresby Jones, 1938

*Ludlow, Shropshire*

BRIAN COOK

**East Anglia**
by Doreen Wallace, 1939

90

**Chiltern Country**
by H.J. Massingham, 1940

*The road to Fingest and Turville, Buckinghamshire*

**English Lakeland**
by Doreen Wallace, 1940

92

**South Eastern Survey**
by Richard Wyndham, 1940
Later re-titled *South East England* (1951)

*The Sussex Weald*

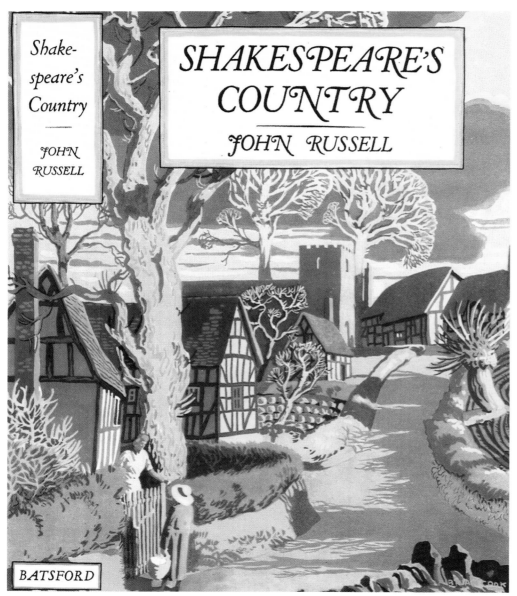

**Shakespeare's Country**
by John Russell, 1942
The design was the first in the series to be restricted to the front and spine.

THE FACE OF BRITAIN

# THE HOME COUNTIES

## By S. P. B. Mais

THE
HOME
COUN-
TIES

S. P. B.
Mais

LONDON
XX
MILES

BATSFORD

BRIAN COOK 1941

**The Home Counties**
by S.P.B. Mais, 1942/3    *An attempt to depict outer suburbia*

**Midland England**
by W.G. Hoskins, 1949

*The village of Wicken, Northamptonshire*

96

THE FACE OF BRITAIN

# NORTH MIDLAND COUNTRY

By J. H. Ingram

NORTH MIDLAND COUNTRY

J. H. Ingram

BATSFORD

**North Midland Country**
by J.H. Ingram, 1947/8

**Wessex**
by Ralph Dutton, 1950

*Worbarrow Bay, Dorset*

98

**Scottish Border Country**

by J.H. Ingram, 1951

*A well-worn specimen*

**Lancashire and the Pennines**
by Frank Singleton, 1952

**The Face of Wales**
by Tudor Edwards, 1950

*The Snowdon Range from Capel Curig*

**Nature in Britain**
with essays by Henry Williamson and others, Crown 8vo, 1936

*One of the 'Pilgrim's Library'*

THE
ISLANDS
OF
IRELAND
By
THOMAS
H.
MASON

# THE ISLANDS OF IRELAND

By Thomas H. Mason

BATSFORD

BRIAN COOK

**The Islands of Ireland**

by Thomas H. Mason, Large 8vo, 1936

## The Islands of Scotland
by Hugh MacDiarmid, 1939

*The islands of Eigg and Rhum off the west coast of Scotland*

*An alternative design showing the Isle of Mull*

**Racing England**
by Patrick R. Chalmers, Large 8vo, 1937

*Ascot Racecourse*

**Hunting England**
by Sir W. Beach Thomas, Large 8vo, 1936

**England and the Farmer**
by H.J. Massingham, Large 8vo, 1941

**Farming England**
by A.G. Street, Large 8vo, 1937

109

**Ancient England**
by Edmund Vale, Large 8vo, 1941

*The Roman wall, Northumberland*

**The Stones of Scotland**
edited by George Scott-Moncrieff, Large Crown 8vo, 1938

*Eilean Donan Castle and Loch Duich*

**Corn Country**
by C. Henry Warren, 1940

**English Woodland**
by John Rodgers, 1941
Watercolour

**British Woodland Trees**
by H.L. Edlin, 1944
An unsuccessful attempt at incorporating the title in the design

**Forestry and Woodland Life**
by H.L. Edlin, 1947

SAILING
AND
CRUISING

By
K. ADLARD
COLES

# SAILING &
CRUISING

FOR THE SMALL BOAT OWNER

By K. Adlard Coles

BATSFORD

BRIAN COOK

**Sailing and Cruising**
by K. Adlard Coles, Large 8vo, 1941
This did not easily fit into any series

BRITAIN'S
MOUNTAIN
HERITAGE

ARTHUR GARDNER

*Britain's Mountain Heritage — Gardner*

BATSFORD

**Britain's Mountain Heritage**
by Arthur Gardner, 1942
A noticeable conventionalization creeping in

**The English Countryside**
A series of essays by H.J. Massingham and others, Crown 8vo, 1939
The first of two jackets

*The Malvern Hills and Bredon from the Cotswold Escarpment*

**The English Countryside**
A pen and wash drawing (opposite) overprinted on Jean Berté process

**The English Countryside**
The pen-and-wash drawing

*Ewelme, Oxfordshire*

**A series of war-time 'Home Front Handbooks', all Crown 8vo, 1940, published at the low price of 3s 6d**

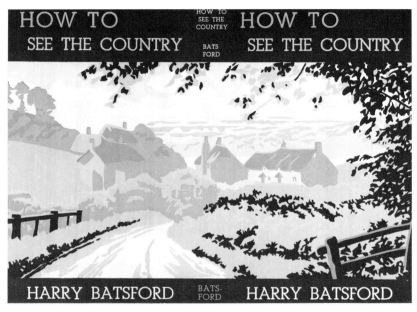

**How to See the Country**
by Harry Batsford

**How to Look at Old Buildings**
by Edmund Vale

**How to See Nature**
by Frances Pitt

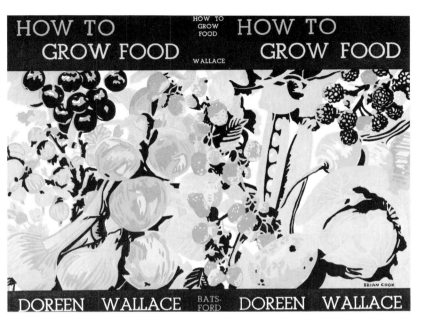

**How to Grow Food**
by Doreen Wallace

**Stuart and Georgian Churches**
by Marcus Whiffen, Demy 8vo, 1949
A different technique involving outlining in pen-and-ink

122

**Come to Britain for Hiking**
A post-war poster for the British Travel and Holidays
Association and a development of the theme of the jacket
of *English Villages and Hamlets* (see page 52).

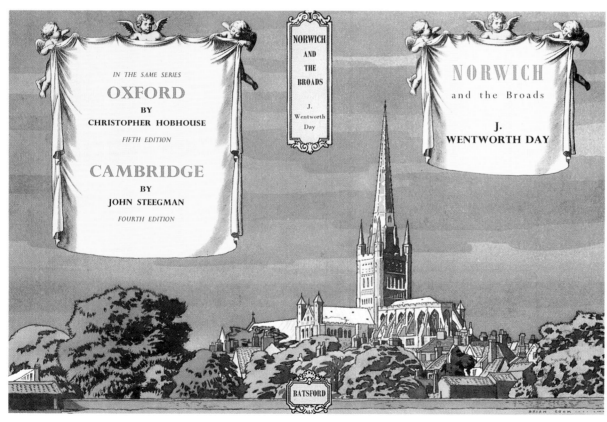

**Norwich and the Broads**
by J. Wentworth-Day, 1953(?)

*Norwich cathedral and city*

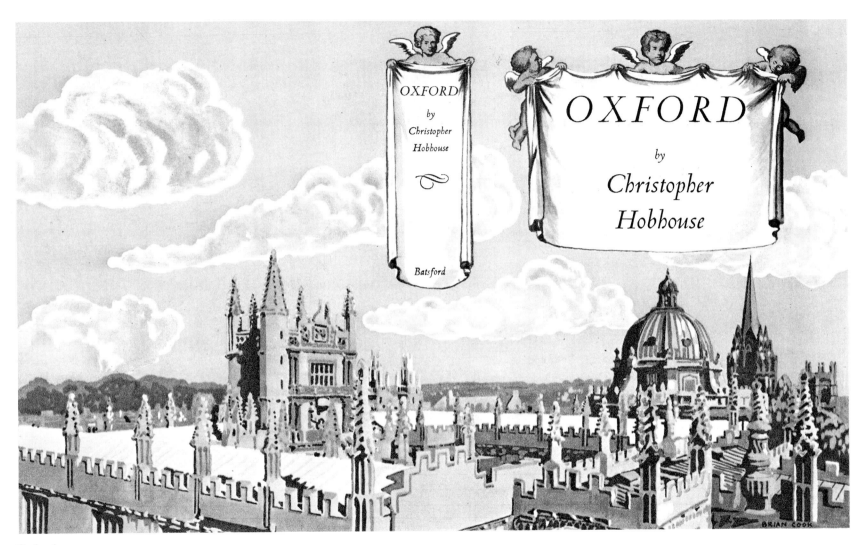

**Oxford**

by Christopher Hobhouse, 1939

The first volume of what later became a series. The author was tragically killed in the early days of the war.

*The towers and spires from All Souls*

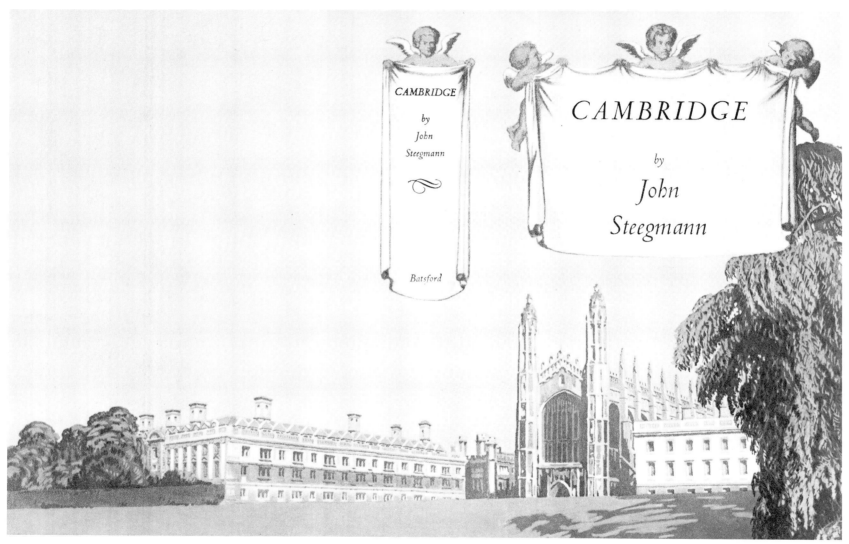

**Cambridge**
by John Steegman, 1940

*King's College Chapel from the Backs*

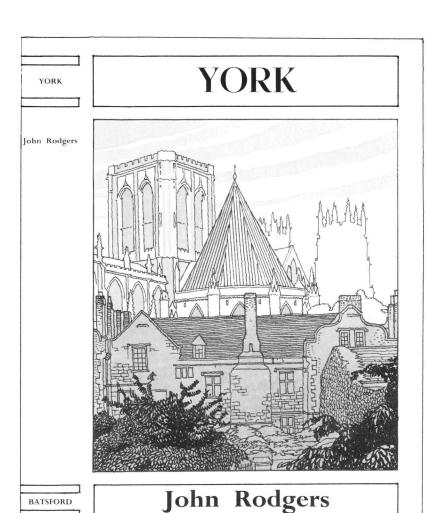

**York**
by John Rodgers, 1951
A post-war series of small volumes. The jackets were first drawn in pen-and-wash and considerable detail. This was then over-printed on Jean Berté colours

**Canterbury**
by William Townsend, 1950

**Salisbury**
by R.L.P. Jowitt, 1951

**CHELTENHAM**

**Bryan Little**

**Cheltenham**
by Bryan Little, 1952

**BRISTOL**

**Tudor Edwards**

**Bristol**
by Tudor Edwards, 1952

**The Cinque Ports**
by R.F. and F.W. Jessup, 1952

**The Three Choirs Cities**
by Bryan Little, 1953

BRIAN COOK

**Interior of St Paul's Cathedral**
A drawing executed for Messrs R.T. Tanner and Co. Ltd.
Pen-and-ink. Date probably late forties

**The Story of the English House**
by Hugh Braun, 1940

*The Georgian house is in Canterbury, Kent*

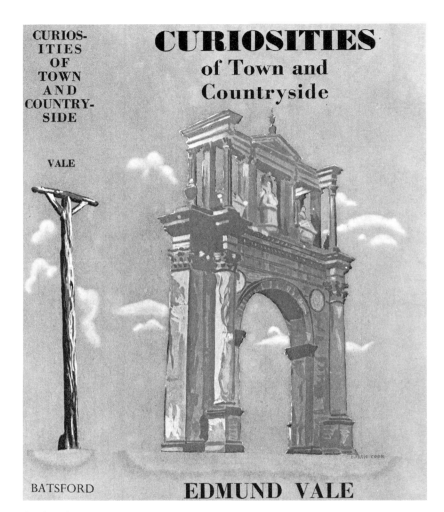

**Curiosities of Town and Countryside**
by Edmund Vale, 1940

**Richard Norman Shaw**
by Sir Reginald Blomfield.
Published shortly before the author died in 1940

BRIAN COOK

*A mediaeval church porch*

**The Styles of English Architecture**

by Arthur Stratton

Originally published in two volumes and subsequently produced in one using the National Gallery subject for the jacket

THE STYLES OF
ENGLISH ARCHITECTURE

ARTHUR STRATTON

*St Martin in the Fields, seen through the portico of the National Gallery*

**British Plants and Their Uses**
by H.L. Edlin, 1951
This ink-and-wash drawing was over-printed on Jean Berté colour

ENG-
LAND
IN
COLOUR

FORD

92
Illustrations
in Colour

# ENGLAND
# IN COLOUR

By Charles Bradley Ford

With 92 Illustrations in Colour

Batsford

**England in Colour**
by Charles Bradley Ford, 1939
Designed to replace the rather unsuccesful first jacket reproduced from a colour
 photograph in 1937 with the title *The Coloured Counties*

**The Face of Ulster**
by Denis O'D. Hanna, 1952

## The Little Guides

A pre-war series published by Messrs. Methuen and Co. Limited and republished after the war jointly by Methuen and Batsford

The Guides were mostly produced on a county basis; 16 were originally planned and four are shown here. The original paintings for most of

**Essex**
by J. Charles Cox, revised by C. Henry Warren

*Finchingfield*

**Surrey**
by J. Charles Cox, revised by E.F. Peeler

*Charlwood*

**Worcestershire**
by F.T.S. Houghton, revised by Matley Moore

*Worcester Cathedral*

**The English Lakes**
by F.G. Gabant, revised by B.L. Thompson

*Ullswater*

# COLLECTORS' CHECKLIST

Listed below are the Batsford books on British topographical subjects which appear with covers by Brian Cook. They are listed by series, although it should be noted that these series were never final or definitive: the arrangement below is based on a broad survey of contemporary Batsford catalogues. Many of the titles were first published in wartime conditions; therefore dates of first publication are approximate. As regards format, the majority of the books were Demy Octavo in size. Those which were larger appear in contemporary catalogues described variously as 'Large Octavo' or 'Medium Octavo': these labels were not used very consistently, and, for the present purposes, 'Large Octavo' has been applied to all of them. Books smaller than Demy Octavo were mostly Crown Octavo, although two series were yet smaller, and will be seen in the lists. The list is complete according to the extant records of the artist and publisher.

## THE ENGLISH LIFE SERIES

Cover designs executed in gouache and printed by Jean Berté.

**The Villages of England**
by A.K. Wickham
First published in 1932, format Large 8vo.
Cover illustrated on page 15. Original painting illustrated on page 45.

**Homes and Gardens of England**
by Harry Batsford and Charles Fry
First published in 1932, format Large 8vo.
Cover illustrated on page 46.

**The Landscape of England**
by Charles Bradley Ford
First published in 1933, format Large 8vo.
Cover illustrated on page 47.

## THE BRITISH HERITAGE SERIES

Cover designs executed in gouache and printed by Jean Berté.

**The Face of Scotland**
by Harry Batsford and Charles Fry
First published in 1933, format Demy 8vo.
Cover illustrated on page 49.

**The Cathedrals of England**
by Harry Batsford and Charles Fry
First published in 1934, format Demy 8vo.
Cover illustrated on page 50.

**The Heart of Scotland**
by George Blake
First published in 1934, format Demy 8vo.
Original painting illustrated on page 51.

**English Villages and Hamlets**
by Humphrey Pakington
First published in 1934, format Demy 8vo.
Original painting illustrated on page 52.

**The Old Inns of England**
by A.E. Richardson
First published in 1934, format Demy 8vo.
Cover illustrated on page 53.

**(The) Parish Churches of England**
by The Rev. J.C. Cox and Charles Bradley Ford
First published in 1934, format Demy 8vo.
Original and later covers illustrated on pages 54 and 55.

**The English Abbey**
by F.H. Crossley
First published in 1935, format Demy 8vo.
Painting for original cover illustrated on page 56.
Later cover illustrated on page 57.

**The English Country House**
by Ralph Dutton
First published in 1935, format Demy 8vo.
Original painting illustrated on page 58.

**The English Garden**
by Ralph Dutton
First published in 1937, format Demy 8vo.
Original painting illustrated on page 59.

**The English Castle**
by Hugh Braun
First published in 1936, format Demy 8vo.
Cover illustrated on page 60.

 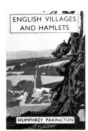

**(The) Old Public Schools of England**
by John Rodgers
First published in 1938, format Demy 8vo.
Cover illustrated on page 61.

**Seas and Shores of England**
by Edmund Vale
First published in 1936, format Demy 8vo.
Cover illustrated on page 62.

**The Countryman's England**
by Dorothy Hartley
First published in 1935, format Demy 8vo.
Original painting illustrated on page 63.

**The Old Towns of England**
by Clive Rouse
First published in 1936, format Demy 8vo.
Original painting illustrated on page 64.

**The Heart of England**
by Ivor Brown
First published in 1935, format Demy 8vo.
Cover (with American publisher's logo) illustrated on page 65. A later edition, with different cover design, appeared in 1951.

**English Village Homes**
by Sydney R. Jones
First published in 1936, format Demy 8vo.
Cover illustrated on page 66.

**The English Cottage**
by Harry Batsford and Charles Fry
First published in 1938, format Demy 8vo.
Cover illustrated on page 67.

**The Land of Wales**
by Eiluned and Peter Lewis
First published in 1937, format Demy 8vo.
Cover illustrated on page 68.

**The Spirit of Ireland**
by Lynn Doyle
First published in 1935, format Demy 8vo.
Original painting illustrated on page 69.

**Old English Customs and Ceremonies**
by F.J. Drake-Carnell
First published in 1938, format Demy 8vo.
Cover illustrated on page 70.

**The Spirit of London**
by Paul Cohen-Portheim
First published in 1935, format Demy 8vo.
Original painting illustrated on page 71.

**Prehistoric England**
by Grahame Clark
First published in 1940, format Demy 8vo.
Cover illustrated on page 72.

**British Hills and Mountains**
by J.H.B. Bell, E.F. Bozman and J. Fairfax Blakeborough
First published in 1940, format Demy 8vo.
Cover illustrated on page 73.

**Old English Household Life**
by Gertrude Jekyll and Sydney R. Jones
This revision of Miss Jekyll's earlier book was first published in 1939, format Demy 8vo.
Cover illustrated on page 74.

**English Church Design 1040 to 1540 A.D.**
by F.H. Crossley
First published in 1945, format Demy 8vo.
Cover illustrated on page 75.

**English Church Craftsmanship**
by F.H. Crossley
First published in 1941, format Demy 8vo.
Cover illustrated on page 76.

**The Greater English Church**
by Harry Batsford and Charles Fry
First published in 1940, format Demy 8vo.
Original painting illustrated on page 77.


# THE FACE OF BRITAIN SERIES

Cover designs executed in gouache and printed by offset lithography, except where otherwise indicated.

**(The) English Downland**
by H.J. Massingham
First published in 1936, format Demy 8vo.
Cover design executed in oils.
Cover illustrated on page 82.

**The Highlands of Scotland**
by Hugh Quigley; photographs by Robert M. Adam
First published in 1936, format Demy 8vo.
Cover design executed in oils.
Cover illustrated on page 83.

**Cotswold Country**
by H.J. Massingham
First published in 1937, format Demy 8vo.
Cover illustrated on page 84.

**North Country**
by Edmund Vale
First published in 1937, format Demy 8vo.
Cover illustrated on page 85.

**The Face of Ireland**
by Michael Floyd
First published in 1937, format Demy 8vo.
Cover design executed in watercolours.
Cover illustrated on page 86.

**The Lowlands of Scotland**
by George Scott-Moncrieff
First published in 1939, format Demy 8vo.
Cover illustrated on page 87.

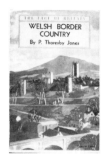

**West Country**
by C. Henry Warren
First published in 1938, format Demy 8vo.
Cover design executed in watercolour.
Cover illustrated on page 88.

**Welsh Border Country**
by P. Thoresby Jones
First published in 1938, format Demy 8vo.
Original painting illustrated on page 89.

**East Anglia**
by Doreen Wallace
First published in 1939, format Demy 8vo.
Cover illustrated on page 90.

**Chiltern Country**
by H.J. Massingham
First published in 1940, format Demy 8vo.
Original painting illustrated on page 91.

**English Lakeland**
by Doreen Wallace
First published in 1940, format Demy 8vo.
Original painting illustrated on page 92.

**South Eastern Survey**
by Richard Wyndham
First published in 1936, format Demy 8vo.
Later (1951) re-titled *South East England*.
Original painting illustrated on page 93.

**Shakespeare's Country**
by John Russell
First published in 1942, format Demy 8vo.
Cover illustrated on page 94.

**The Home Counties**
by S.P.B. Mais
First published in 1942/3, format Demy 8vo.
Cover illustrated on page 95.

**Midland England**
by W.G. Hoskins
First published in 1949, format Demy 8vo.
Cover illustrated on page 96.

**North Midland Country**
by J.H. Ingram
First published in 1947/8, format Demy 8vo.
Cover illustrated on page 97.

**The Heart of The English Midlands**
by J.H. Ingram
First published in 1947/8, format Demy 8vo.

**Wessex**
by Ralph Dutton
First published in 1950, format Demy 8vo.
Original painting illustrated on page 98.

**Lincolnshire and The Fens**
by M.W. Barley
First published in 1952, format Demy 8vo.
Original painting illustrated on page 98.

**Scottish Border Country**
by F.R. Banks
First published in 1951, format Demy 8vo.
Cover illustrated on page 99.

 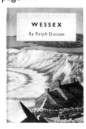

**Lancashire and The Pennines**
by Frank Singleton
First published in 1952, format Demy 8vo.
Original painting illustrated on page 100.

**Geology and Scenery in Britain**
by T.G. Miller
First published in 1953, format Demy 8vo.
Original painting illustrated on page 101.
Not published originally as one of *The Face of Britain*
series, it was on occasion marketed as such.

**The Face of Wales**
by Tudor Edwards
First published in 1950, format Demy 8vo.
Original painting illustrated on page 102.

 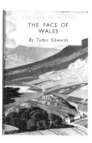

## THE PILGRIM'S LIBRARY

**The Beauty of Britain**
Introduction by J.B. Priestley
First published in 1935; this jacket appeared in 1937,
format Crown 8vo.
Cover design executed in gouache, printed by Jean Berté.
Cover illustrated on page 78.

**The Legacy of England**
A collection of essays
First published in 1935, format Crown 8vo.
Cover executed in scraperboard overprinted on
Jean Berté.
Cover illustrated on page 79.

**Nature in Britain**
with essays by Henry Williamson and others
First published in 1936, format Crown 8vo.
Cover illustrated on page 103.

**The English Countryside**
with essays by H.J. Massingham and others
First published in 1939, format Crown 8vo.
There were two covers: the later version was executed
in pen-and-wash, overprinted on Jean Berté.
Cover and original painting illustrated on pages 118
and 119.

## HOME FRONT HANDBOOKS

**How to See the Country**
by Harry Batsford
First published in 1940, format Crown 8vo.
Cover illustrated on page 120.

**How to Look at Old Buildings**
by Edmund Vale
First published in 1940, format Crown 8vo.
Cover illustrated on page 120.

**How to See Nature**
by Frances Pitt
First published in 1940, format Crown 8vo.
Cover illustrated on page 121.

**How to Grow Food**
by Doreen Wallace
First published in 1940, format Crown 8vo.
Cover illustrated on page 121.

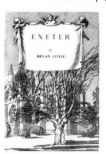 

## THE BRITISH CITIES SERIES

**Norwich and the Broads**
by J. Wentworth Day
First published in 1953(?), format Demy 8vo.
Cover illustrated on page 124.

**Exeter**
by Bryan Little
First published in 1953, format Demy 8vo.

**Oxford**
by Christopher Hobhouse
First published in 1939, format Demy 8vo.
Cover illustrated on page 125.

**Cambridge**
by John Steegman
First published in 1940, format Demy 8vo.
Cover illustrated on page 126.

The remaining volumes in this series all featured cover designs executed in pen-and-wash and overprinted on Jean Berté.

**York**
by John Rodgers
First published in 1951, format Crown 8vo.
Cover and original painting illustrated on page 127.

**Canterbury**
by William Townsend
First published in 1950, format Crown 8vo.
Original painting illustrated on page 128.

**Salisbury**
by R.L.P. Jowitt
First published in 1951, format Crown 8vo.
Original painting illustrated on page 128.

**The Isle of Wight**
by R.L.P. and Dorothy M. Jowitt
First published in 1951, format Crown 8vo.

**Cheltenham**
by Bryan Little
First published in 1952, format Crown 8vo.
Cover illustrated on page 129.

**Bristol**
by Tudor Edwards
First published in 1952, format Crown 8vo.
Cover illustrated on page 129.

**The Cinque Ports**
by R.F. and F.W. Jessup
First published in 1952, format Crown 8vo.
Cover illustrated on page 130.

**The Three Choirs Cities**
by Bryan Little
First published in 1953, format Crown 8vo.
Cover illustrated on page 130.

# THE LITTLE GUIDES

Published jointly by Methuen & Co. Ltd and B.T. Batsford Ltd, *c.*1950. All designs executed in gouache and printed by offset lithography. The originals of most of the jacket designs were discovered too late for reproduction in this book.

**Essex**
by J. Charles Cox, revised by C. Henry Warren
Cover illustrated on page 138.

**Surrey**
by J. Charles Cox, revised by E.F. Peeler
Cover illustrated on page 138.

**Worcestershire**
by F.T.S. Houghton, revised by Matley Moore
Cover illustrated on page 139.

**The English Lakes**
by F.G. Gabant, revised by B.L. Thompson
Original painting illustrated on page 139.

Some further titles in this series included **Buckinghamshire, Cornwall, Derbyshire, Devonshire, Dorset, Gloucestershire, Hampshire, Kent, Norfolk, Somerset, Suffolk** and **Wiltshire**. Some of these titles are illustrated below.

# MISCELLANEOUS

**The Islands of Scotland**
by Hugh MacDiarmid
First published in 1939, format Large 8vo.
Cover design executed in gouache, printed by offset lithography.
Original painting (and alternative design) illustrated on page 105.

**The Islands of Ireland**
by Thomas H. Mason
First published in 1936, format Demy 8vo.
Cover design executed in gouache, printed by offset lithography.
Cover illustrated on page 104.

**The Islands of England**
by J.H. Ingram
First published in 1952, format Large 8vo.
Cover design executed in gouache, printed by offset lithography.

**Racing England**
by Patrick R. Chalmers
First published in 1937, format Large 8vo.
Cover illustrated on page 106.

**Hunting England**
by Sir W. Beach Thomas
First published in 1936, format Large 8vo.
Original painting illustrated on page 107.

**England and the Farmer**
by H.J. Massingham
First published in 1941, format Demy 8vo.
Original painting illustrated on page 108.

**Farming England**
by A.G. Street
First published in 1937, format Demy 8vo.
Original painting illustrated on page 109.

**Ancient England**
by Edmund Vale
First published in 1941, format Demy 8vo.
Original painting illustrated on page 110.

**The Stones of Scotland**
edited by George Scott-Moncrieff
First published in 1938, format Large 8vo.
Original painting illustrated on page 111.

**Corn Country**
by C. Henry Warren
First published in 1940, format Demy 8vo.
Original painting illustrated on page 112.

**English Woodland**
by John Rodgers
First published in 1941, format Demy 8vo.
Cover design executed in watercolour, printed by offset lithography
Original painting illustrated on page 113.

**British Woodland Trees**
by H.L. Edlin
First published in 1944, format Demy 8vo.
Cover illustrated on page 114.

**Forestry and Woodland Life**
by H.L. Edlin
First published in 1947, format Demy 8vo.
Cover illustrated on page 115.

**Sailing and Cruising** (for the small boat owner)
by K. Adlard Coles
First published in 1937, format Demy 8vo.
Cover illustrated on page 116.

**Britain's Mountain Heritage**
by Arthur Gardner
First published in 1942, format Demy 8vo.
Cover illustrated on page 117.

**Stuart and Georgian Churches**
by Marcus Whiffen
First published in 1947/8, format Demy 8vo.
Original painting illustrated on page 122.

**Story of the English House**
by Hugh Braun
First published in 1940, format Large 8vo.
Cover illustrated on page 132.

**Curiosities of Town and Countryside**
by Edmund Vale
First published in 1940, format Demy 8vo.
Cover illustrated on page 132.

**Richard Norman Shaw**
by Sir Reginald Blomfield
First published in 1940, format Demy 8vo.
Cover illustrated on page 133.

**The Styles of English Architecture**
by Arthur Stratton
First published in c.1934, format Demy 8vo.
Two original designs illustrated on page 134.

**British Plants and Their Uses**
by H.L. Edlin
First published in 1951, format Demy 8vo.
Cover design executed in ink-and-wash, overprinted on Jean Berté.
Original painting illustrated on page 135.

**England in Colour**
by Charles Bradley Ford
First published with this title in 1939, format Demy 8vo.
Cover illustrated on page 136.

**The Face of Ulster**
by Denis O'D. Hanna
First published in 1952, format Demy 8vo, a post-war echo of the *Face of Britain* series.
Original painting illustrated on page 137.

**London Work and Play**
Introduction by Harry Batsford
First published in 1950, format $8^{7}/_{10} \times 6^{3}/_{8}$".
Original painting illustrated on page 41.